The Littlest Book of England

Edited and illustrated by
Julia Killingback

Ragged Bears

Dedicated to Bob and Sheilah

O, to be in England
Now that April's there,
And whoever wakes in England
Sees, some morning, unaware,
That the lowest boughs
             and the brushwood sheaf
Round the elm-tree bole are in tiny leaf,
While the chaffinch sings
             on the orchard bough
In England – now!

                          Robert Browning

This royal throne of kings,

                    this scepter'd isle,
This earth of majesty, this seat of Mars,
This other Eden, demi paradise,
This fortress built by Nature for herself
Against infection and the hand of war,
This happy breed of men, this little world,
This precious stone set in the silver sea ...

                    William Shakespeare

Stratford-on-Avon

Pile of Stonehenge! So
   proud to hint yet keep
Thy secrets, thou that
   lov'st to stand and hear
The Plain resounding
   to the whirlwind's sweep,
Inmate of lonesome
   Nature's endless year ...

William Wordsworth

Stonehenge

I wandered lonely as a cloud
That floats on high o'er vales and hills,
When all at once I saw a crowd,
A host, of golden daffodils;
Beside the lake, beneath the trees,
Fluttering and dancing in the breeze.

William Wordsworth

Grasmere – Lake District

There is a spot mid barren hills
Where winter howls and drives the rain …
… the house is old, the trees are bare,
Moonless above bends twilight's dome …
… the mute bird sitting on the stone,
The dank moss dripping from the wall,
The thorn trees gaunt, the walks
                              o'ergrown
I love them, how I love them all.

                              Emily Brontë

Haworth, Yorkshire

The boats, the sands, the esplanade
The laughing crowd;
Light-hearted, loud
Greetings from some not ill-endowed;
The evening sunlit cliffs, the talk
Hailings and halts,
The keen sea-salts,
The band, the Morgenblätter waltz.

Thomas Hardy

Weymouth

But let my due feet never fail,
To walk the studious Cloysters pale,
And love the high embowed Roof,
With antick Pillars massy proof,
And storied Windows richly dight,
Casting a dimm religious light.
There let the pealing Organ blow,
To the full voic'd Quire below,
In Service high, and Anthems cleer,
As may with sweetnes, through mine ear
Dissolve me into extasies,
And bring all Heav'n before mine eyes.

John Milton

York

Each rural sight, each sound,
   each smell, combine;
The tinkling sheep-bell,
   or the breath of kine;
The new-mown hay
   that scents the swelling breeze,
Or cottage-chimney smoking
   thro' the trees.
The chilling night-dews fall:
   away, retire;
For see, the glow-worm lights
   her amorous fire!

                              Gilbert White

Selborne

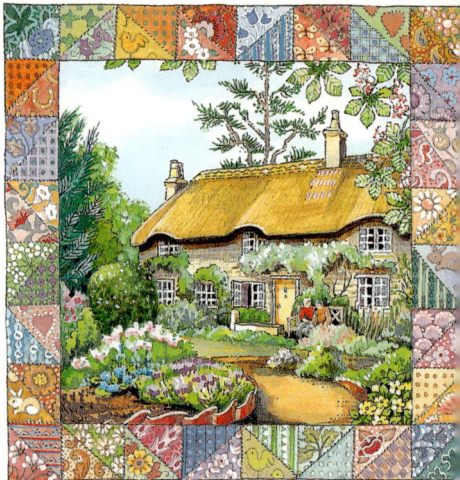

This is the weather the cuckoo likes,
And so do I;
When showers betumble the chestnut spikes,
And nestlings fly;
And the little brown nightingale bills his best,
And they sit outside at "The Travellers Rest",
And maidens come forth sprig-muslin drest,
And citizens dream of the south and west,
And so do I.

Thomas Hardy

Dorset

Our England is a garden that is full of
    stately views,
Of borders, beds, and shrubberies,
    and lawns, and avenues,
With statues on the terraces
    and peacocks strutting by;
But the glory of the garden lies in more
    than meets the eye.

Rudyard Kipling

Kew

© 1995 Ragged Bears Ltd.,
Andover, Hampshire SP11 9HX.
in association with arsEdition, CH-6301 Zug
All rights reserved · Printed in Germany
ISBN 1 85714 080 X

The Littlest Books Collection

The Littlest Christmas Book
The Littlest Book for a Joyful Event
The Littlest Book for Every Day
The Littlest Book for Mother's Day
The Littlest Book for the Heart
The Littlest Book for Your Birthday
The Littlest Book Just for You
The Littlest Book of Bears
The Littlest Book of Birds
The Littlest Book of Castles
The Littlest Book of Cats and Mice
The Littlest Book of Ireland
The Littlest Book of Kittens
The Littlest Book of London
The Littlest Book of Mice